Trumbler Wells 20052   11-5-85 $9.70

Snakes

Experts on child reading levels
have consulted on the level of text and
concepts in this book.

At the end of the book is a "Look Back and Find" section
which provides additional information and encourages
the child to refer back to previous pages
for the answers to the questions posed.

Angela Grunsell trained as a teacher in 1969.
She has a Diploma in Reading and Related Skills
and for the last five years has advised London
teachers on materials and resources.
She works for the ILEA as an advisory teacher in
primary schools in Hackney, London.

Published in the United States in 1984 by
Franklin Watts, 387 Park Avenue South, New York, NY 10016

© Aladdin Books Ltd/Franklin Watts

Designed and produced by
Aladdin Books Ltd, 70 Old Compton Street, London W1
ISBN 0 531 04901 9
Library of Congress Catalog
Card Number: 84 51811
Printed in Belgium

FRANKLIN · WATTS · FIRST · LIBRARY

Snakes

by
Kate Petty

Consultant
Angela Grunsell

Illustrated by
Alan Baker

Franklin Watts
London · New York · Toronto · Sydney

Have you ever touched a snake?
Their scaly skins are dry and not slimy at all.
A few snakes are poisonous, but most of them,
like these Grass Snakes, are harmless.

Snakes lay eggs.
Some of the babies have a tiny "egg tooth"
to help them break out of the shell.
They can look after themselves right away.

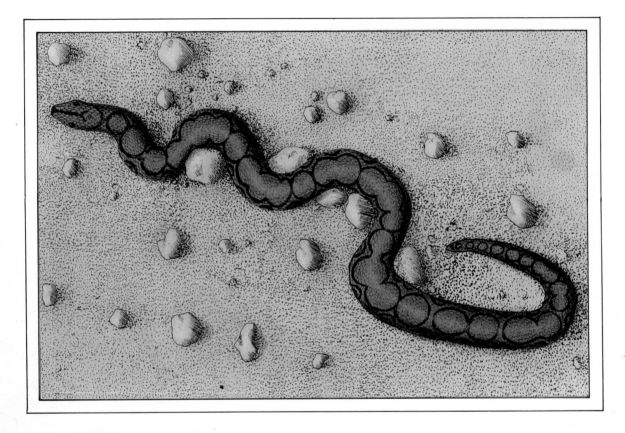

Snakes have no legs but they can move at
great speed. They curve their way along,
pushing their strong bodies against
rough surfaces as they go.

This enormous Anaconda can swim and
climb trees too. It is 18 feet long and
one of the biggest snakes.
Anacondas live by rivers in South America.

Snakes have to hunt and kill other animals
for their food. The Boa Constrictor
coils around its prey and squeezes –
or constricts – until it stops breathing.

Boas are very beautiful snakes.
These two come from South America.
The Emerald Boa lives in trees and hunts
parrots and monkeys.

Pythons are constrictors too. This one
is the largest snake of all. It is
a full-grown Reticulated Python, measuring
27 feet long. It is found in parts of Asia.

12

Mother pythons coil around their eggs until they hatch. During this time they don't eat. This African Rock Python can survive for two years between meals.

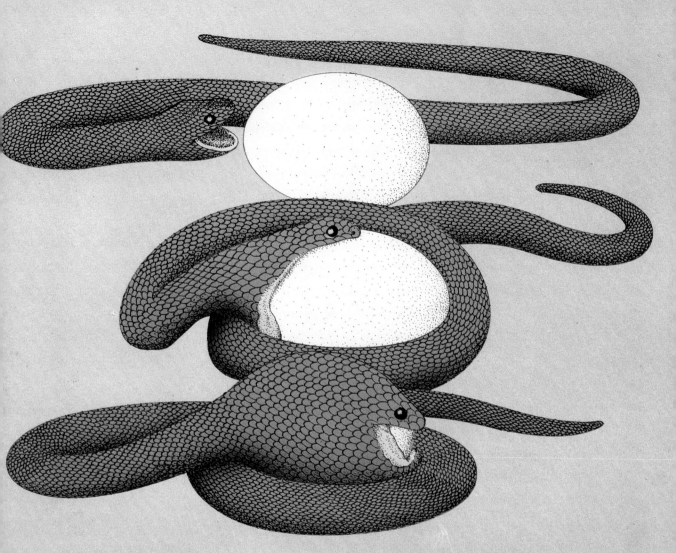

Snakes' jawbones are specially hinged
so they can swallow large objects.
When the African Egg-eating Snake has finished
eating the egg, it spits out the shell.

A snake uses its flickering tongue to test
the air for scents of other animals. It is the bite
of a poisonous snake which is dangerous.
The poison is injected through its fangs.

Cobras are poisonous snakes.
The King Cobra is so large and dangerous
it will attack humans and even elephants.
The Indian Cobra here is smaller.

The little mongoose is the snake's enemy.
It confuses the Cobra by running around it
in circles. Then it darts in and bites
the snake's neck before it can strike.

These two snakes from Africa are also
members of the cobra family.
Black-necked Cobras spit their venom.
Their victims can be blinded by it.

The Black Mamba is small and deadly.
It lives in the branches of trees.
The poisonous bite of a Mamba can
kill a human in ten minutes.

Vipers are another family of poisonous snakes.
Their fangs are so long that they fold in
when the viper's mouth is shut.
This European Viper is usually called an Adder.

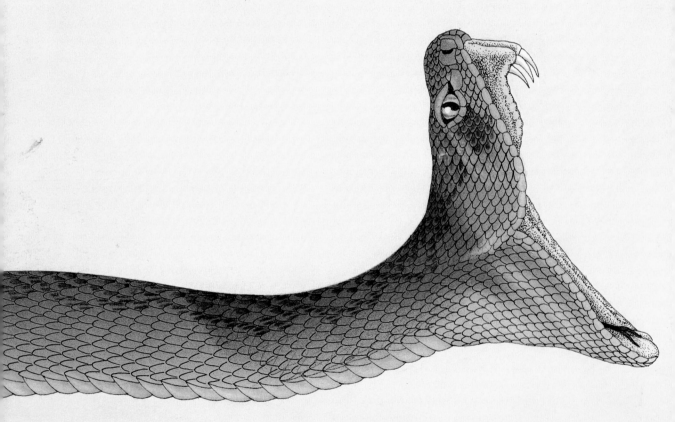

The Puff Adder from Africa has bold markings which warn other animals to keep away. It puffs up its body and hisses if they come near.

Pit vipers have hollows or "pits" in their cheeks,
that are sensitive to heat.
This Bushmaster can stay in hiding until
it feels the warmth of its victims close by.

Rattlesnakes are pit vipers. They are found all over the United States. Can you see the "rattle" at the end of the Diamond-backed Rattlesnake's tail?

Snakes protect themselves in different ways.
The Sidewinder Rattlesnake can hide very
quickly by covering itself with sand.
This also protects it from the fierce desert sun.

This harmless Scarlet King Snake is protected because it has a poisonous twin. A hawk flying overhead will mistake the markings for those of a dangerous Coral Snake and leave it alone.

As you get bigger you outgrow your clothes.
A snake outgrows its skin!
It sheds its complete outer skin
several times a year.

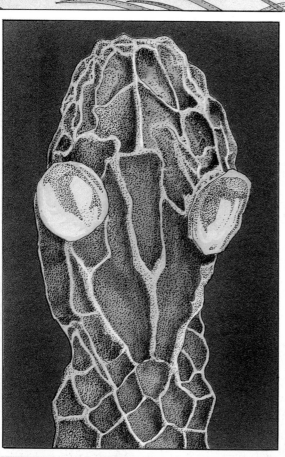

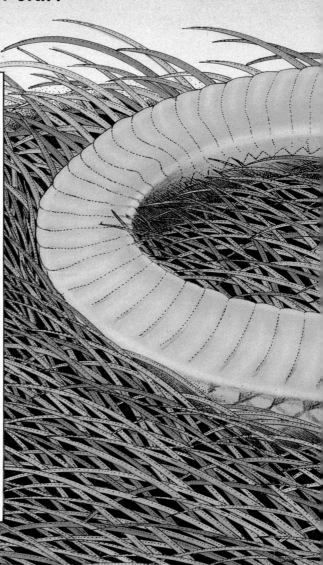

A snake might live to be fifteen years old,
but many are killed before they reach this age.
This Hognosed Snake is pretending to be dead
so that nothing will attack it.

Look back and find

What other animals lay eggs?

Why might you expect snakes to lay eggs?

Do all snakes come from eggs?
No. Some sorts of snake "hatch" while they are still inside their mothers, so they are born live.

Is the Python a poisonous snake?

Why do snakes have to kill other animals?

Where does this Python live?

What does a snake use its tongue for?

What are fangs?

Do all snakes have their fangs at the front?
Cobras are front-fanged, so are vipers. A group of snakes called "colubrids" are back-fanged. Very few colubrids are venomous.

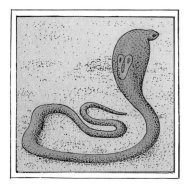

How does the Cobra behave when it is alarmed?
*It rears up and spreads its "hood." As it
prepares to strike it sways from side to side.*

How does the mongoose confuse the Cobra?

Where might you find a European Viper?
*These snakes are found all over Europe,
including Britain.*

What happens if you are bitten by one?
*It would make you very ill. You should
get help right away.*

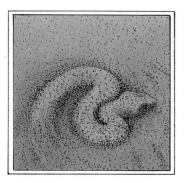

What is the Sidewinder doing?

Why does it need to stay cool?
*Snakes are coldblooded creatures.
They don't like to get too hot or too cold.*

How did the Sidewinder get its name?
It travels sideways across the sand.

Index

PRINTED IN BELGIUM BY

proost

INTERNATIONAL BOOK PRODUCTION